Most Popular
North American Animals

Billy Grinslott & Kinsey Marie Books

ISBN - 9781965098615

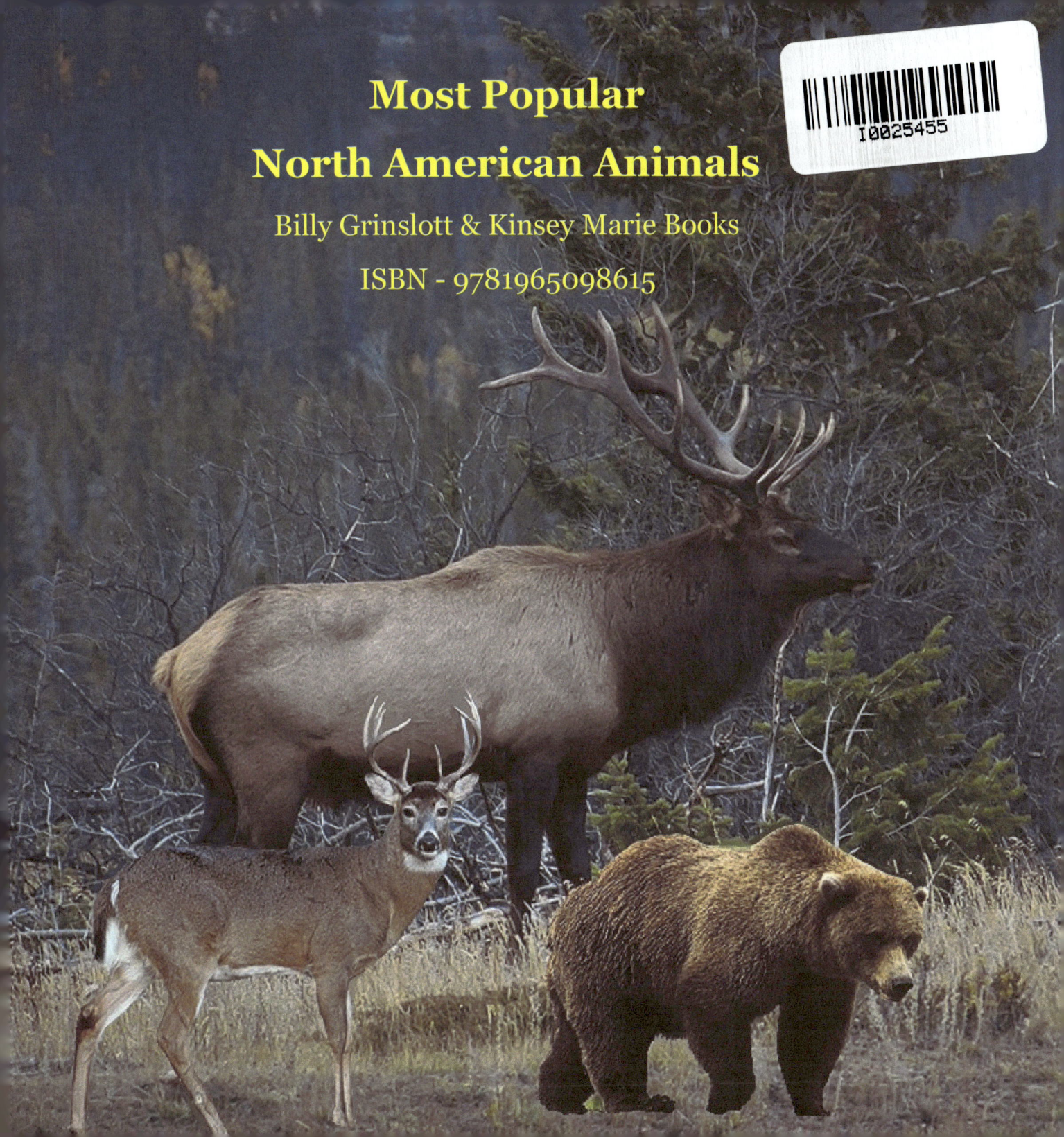

Chipmunks are found in many areas. Chipmunks are small members of the squirrel family. They like to eat nuts and seeds. Chipmunks are most active during the day, especially at dawn and dusk. They have pouches inside of their cheeks so they can carry food. They are very friendly and will take food from your hand. Chipmunks need about 15 hours of sleep per day. The smallest chipmunk species is Tamias minimus, which is found throughout North America.

There are many squirrels in the wild. You may see a red or gray squirrel. The most popular is the gray squirrel. Squirrels are very acrobatic and can climb trees. Their favorite food is acorns. Squirrels hide their food in many small stashes and can find more than 90% of them later. Squirrels are fast and can run up a tree at 12 miles per hour. Newborn squirrels are blind, deaf, and hairless, and rely on their mother until they mature.

There are many types of rabbits in the wild. The most common is the cottontail. Rabbits are cute, friendly, and fun to watch. Many people have rabbits for pets. They have soft fluffy fur. They are called cottontails because they have a white fluffy tail that looks like a cotton ball.

The hare is bigger than a rabbit with longer ears and legs. Their longs legs help them to run fast. They are agile and faster than most rabbits. Hares have excellent hearing and vision. Hares have large ears and eyes that are positioned on the sides of their head, giving them a wide field of vision. Hares can change color. Hares have the ability to change color depending on the season and their surroundings.

Opossums or possums have strong tails and can hang from trees. One trick that a possum has, is when it feels danger is it will play dead. It will lay there and not move. Possums have white to gray face hair. Possums like to eat wood ticks. They are also immune to snakebites. Opossums are susceptible to frostbite because their hands and tails are not protected by fur. Opossums are marsupials, which means they have pouches for their young, like kangaroos and koalas.

Raccoons like to come out at night. Their eyes are made so they can see in the dark. Raccoons are highly intelligent and can solve problems. They can learn to open doors, trash cans, and other containers. They are called masked bandits because they like to raid and eat out of trash cans at night. Raccoons can survive in many environments.

Ringtails look like a racoon. They have stripes on their tails, but their face more resembles a cat. They are a member of the racoon family. Ringtails can be found in some parts of North America. Ringtails are excellent climbers capable of ascending vertical walls, trees, rocky cliffs and even cactus. They are mostly nocturnal. Ringtails are agile climbers and leapers, with hind legs that can rotate 180 degrees. Their long tails help with balance. Ringtails have anal glands that produce a foul-smelling secretion.

Fishers live in the forests of Canada and the northern United States. They hiss and growl when upset. They are closely related to badgers, mink, and otters. Fisher young are known as kits. Fishers are one of the few animals that eat porcupines. Fishers are also called pekan, pequam, wejack, and woolang.

Prairie dogs live in family groups called coteries, which are made up of one male, several females, and their young. Their vocabulary is more advanced than any other animal language. They got their name because they live on the prairies and their warning calls which sound like dog barks. They build mounds around their den to keep water out. Prairie dogs are small burrowing mammals that are related to squirrels.

Groundhogs or woodchucks are the largest member of the squirrel family. Groundhogs get their name because of their big bodies, and they live underground. Groundhogs are skilled climbers and swimmers. Groundhogs are true hibernators, sleeping for up to six months. Groundhog Day is where Punxsutawney Phil predicts how long winter will last.

Beavers use their teeth to cut and knock down trees. They build dams with them to block water, so they have a place to live and swim. They also eat wood. Beavers can stay underwater for about 8 minutes. Beavers slap their tails on the water to indicate danger. Beavers are the largest rodents in North America.

Otters have the thickest fur of any animal. The otter is one of the few mammals that use tools, like rocks to break thing open. A group of otters resting together is called a raft.

Otters primarily rely on their sense of touch, whiskers, and forepaws, in murky waters to locate food. Otters have built in pouches of loose skin under their forearms to stash extra food when diving.

Pikas are small mammals with short, round ears and hind legs that are slightly shorter than their front legs. They are brown and black in color. Pikas live in boulder fields on mountain peaks, in rocky areas, and in treeless slopes. Pikas are active during the day and are territorial about their dens and surrounding area. They are vocal animals that use sharp calls or whistles to warn others of danger. Pikas eat plants such as thistle, sedges, wildflowers, and grasses. They store their food for winter in piles called haystacks or hay piles.

Black-footed ferrets have a strip of dark fur across their eyes that makes them look like they are wearing a mask. The black-footed ferret is the only ferret that is native to America. Black-footed ferrets were thought to be extinct twice. They were rediscovered in Wyoming in 1981. Black-footed ferrets are playful. Black-footed ferrets are agile climbers. Black-footed ferrets have been reintroduced to Montana, South Dakota, Wyoming, and other states.

Stoats have very good eyesight, good hearing and a strong sense of smell. They hunt day and night and can travel up to 20 miles per hour and cover large areas in a short time. Stoats are good at climbing trees to steal baby birds and eggs. Stoats fur color changes to white in the winter so they can blend into the snow. Baby stoats are called kits and are born in the spring. They are born blind, deaf, toothless, and covered in soft fur called down.

Javelinas live in large family groups led by a dominant male. Other members of the group are ranked by their size, with larger animals having higher status. Javelinas are mainly vegetarian and eat a variety of desert plants, including cactus, agave, mesquite beans, and prickly pear. An adult javelina can reach a weight of fifty-five pounds. The javelina usually is not aggressive unless threatened, then it will open its mouth wide and loudly pops its teeth together. Javelinas can run up to 25 miles per hour and ump 6 feet. Baby javelinas are called reds, because they have red fur when they're young.

Bobcats are named for their short, bobbed tails with white tips. They have similar markings to lynxes but are much smaller. Bobcats live in a variety of habitats. Bobcats are skilled at leaping and can run up to 30 miles per hour.

The Lynx is larger than the bobcat and has lighter fur and more spots. The lynx is more than twice the size of a house cat. Lynx have natural snowshoes for feet because they have long hair on their feet. Lynx like to hunt at night. They have excellent hearing and eyesight, and can spot a mouse from 250 feet away. Lynx have colors that help them blend into their surroundings. Each lynx has a different pattern, similar to a human fingerprint.

The cougar has a number of different names, it's also known as the mountain lion. They are the fourth largest cat in the world. The cougar has the largest range of any wild cat in the North America. A cougar can jump upward 18 feet from a sitting position. They can leap up to 30 feet horizontally. Cougars cannot roar like a lion, but they can make calls like a human scream.

The bighorn sheep is part of the sheep family and likes to live in mountainous areas. Females are called ewes and males are called rams. They are called rams because they like to use their horns to slam into things. Their horn size is a symbol of how high they rank in the herd. The bigger their horns are, the higher they rank. Their large curled horns that can weigh up to 30 pounds. Bighorn sheep are excellent climbers and can stand on ledges as narrow as 2 inches.

Mountain goats can jump 12 feet in one leap. They like to live in high altitude environments. A mountain goats fur coat has a double layer that sheds in the summer and provides warmth in the winter. They have hooves designed to grip onto rocks to keep from falling. Both male and female mountain goats have horns. You can tell a mountain goat's age by counting the rings on its horns.

There are several types of antelopes, this one is known as the pronghorn. Antelopes have extremely developed senses which help them detect danger. They are quick runners and can run up to 60 mph. They can maintain high speeds for longer periods of time than cheetahs. They all like to live in herds. Antelopes don't outrun other animals. They out maneuver them. They can twist and turn very quickly. They are related to cows, sheep, and goats.

The whitetail deer is the most popular deer in North America. Whitetail deer have good eyesight and hearing. They can detect small sounds from a quarter of a mile away. Only male deer grow antlers, which are shed each year. Whitetail deer are good swimmers and will use large streams and lakes to escape predators. A young deer is called a fawn, a male is a buck, and a female is called a doe. They are the most common deer species and live everywhere in North America.

Elk are the second largest members of the deer family. Bulls can weigh up to 1,100 lbs. Elk antlers can grow up to an inch per day. They can run 40 miles per hour and outrun horses. Elk have a good sense of hearing and can swivel their ears back and forth. Elk have eyes on the sides of their heads and can see in every direction except directly in front or behind. They make a cool bugling sound when communicating with other elk. It's fun to listen to them.

Caribou are also known as reindeer. Both male and female reindeer grow antlers. Reindeer are covered in hair from their nose to the bottom of their hooves. They have large, hollow hooves that help them walk on snow and dig for food. Reindeer have hair completely covering their nose. Reindeer are the only deer species to be widely domesticated. Santa uses Reindeer to pull his slay. Rudolph the reindeer is the most popular of the reindeer.

There are six different subspecies of moose. Moose are built for cold areas and like living in cold regions with snow. Moose are the largest members of the deer family. Moose are huge and weigh up to 1500 pounds. Moose love water and are good swimmers. Moose have poor eyesight but compensate with a good sense of smell and hearing. At 5 days old they can outrun a person.

Kit foxes are native to much of the western United States and northern Mexico. Kit foxes are the smallest foxes in North America, weighing only about five pounds.. Despite their slender size, they have large ears to help aid their hearing and to dissipate heat. Kit foxes are mainly active at night and resting in their dens during the day. kit foxes can survive without fresh water, by getting all their fluids from their food.

Red foxes have excellent hearing, allowing them to hear rodents digging underground from miles away. When afraid, red foxes grin or look like they are smiling. Red foxes front paws have five toes, while their hind feet only have four. Foxes dig underground dens where they raise their kits and hide from predators. A group of foxes is called a skulk or a leash. Babys are called kits and females are called vixens.

The coyote is bigger than a fox weighing between 20 and 45 pounds. Eastern coyotes are part wolf. Coyotes are great for pest control. They like to eat mice and rats. They can adapt and live almost anywhere, even in the city. Coyotes are very smart and have been observed learning and following traffic signals in some cities. They have a yip type of call when they communicate with each other. Coyotes are found in all the United States, except Hawaii.

Wolves, coyotes, and foxes are all part of the dog family. The timber wolf, also known as the gray wolf, is the largest wolf in North America. Wolves are legendary because of their spine-tingling howl, which they use to communicate. Each wolf has its own unique howl. Wolves are born deaf and blind, but their senses develop at about two weeks. They like to roam in packs of 2 to 25 wolves. Their territory size is 25 to 150 square miles. You can see gray and red wolves in many areas of North America.

Arctic wolves have two thick layers of fur. The outer layer gets thicker in the winter months. As a result, their body temperature can stay warm enough even when it is bitter cold outside. Arctic wolves have white fur all year which allows them to blend into their snowy surroundings. They have fur on the paws to insulate them from snow and ice and it also provides for a better grip on slippery surfaces. Arctic wolves have keen senses of sight, hearing, and smell. Arctic wolves live in packs of just a couple members to about twenty.

Black bears are the smallest members of the bear family in North America. Black Bears love to eat sweet things like berries, fruits, and vegetables. They are good climbers and fast runners. They are excellent swimmers and can paddle at least a mile and a half in freshwater. They usually sleep for long periods of time and hibernate during the winter. They typically try to stay away from people unless they find food in the area.

Brown bears are often called Grizzley bears, but they're not. Brown bears can be up to seven feet tall and weigh up to 700 pounds for males and 350 pounds for females. Brown bears eat mostly grass, roots, and berries but will eat fish and other small mammals. They are silent but can communicate with grunts, roars, or squeals.

Grizzly bears are a subspecies of the brown bear. They are called Grizzly bears because they have silver or lighter colored tips on their hair, a grizzled look. The hump on a Grizzly bear's back is a huge muscle. Grizzly bears don't hibernate like other bears. They are highly intelligent, have excellent memories and great smell. They are good swimmers and fast runners. They can run up to 35 miles per hour for short sprints. Grizzly bears are apex predators, meaning they are at the top of the food chain.

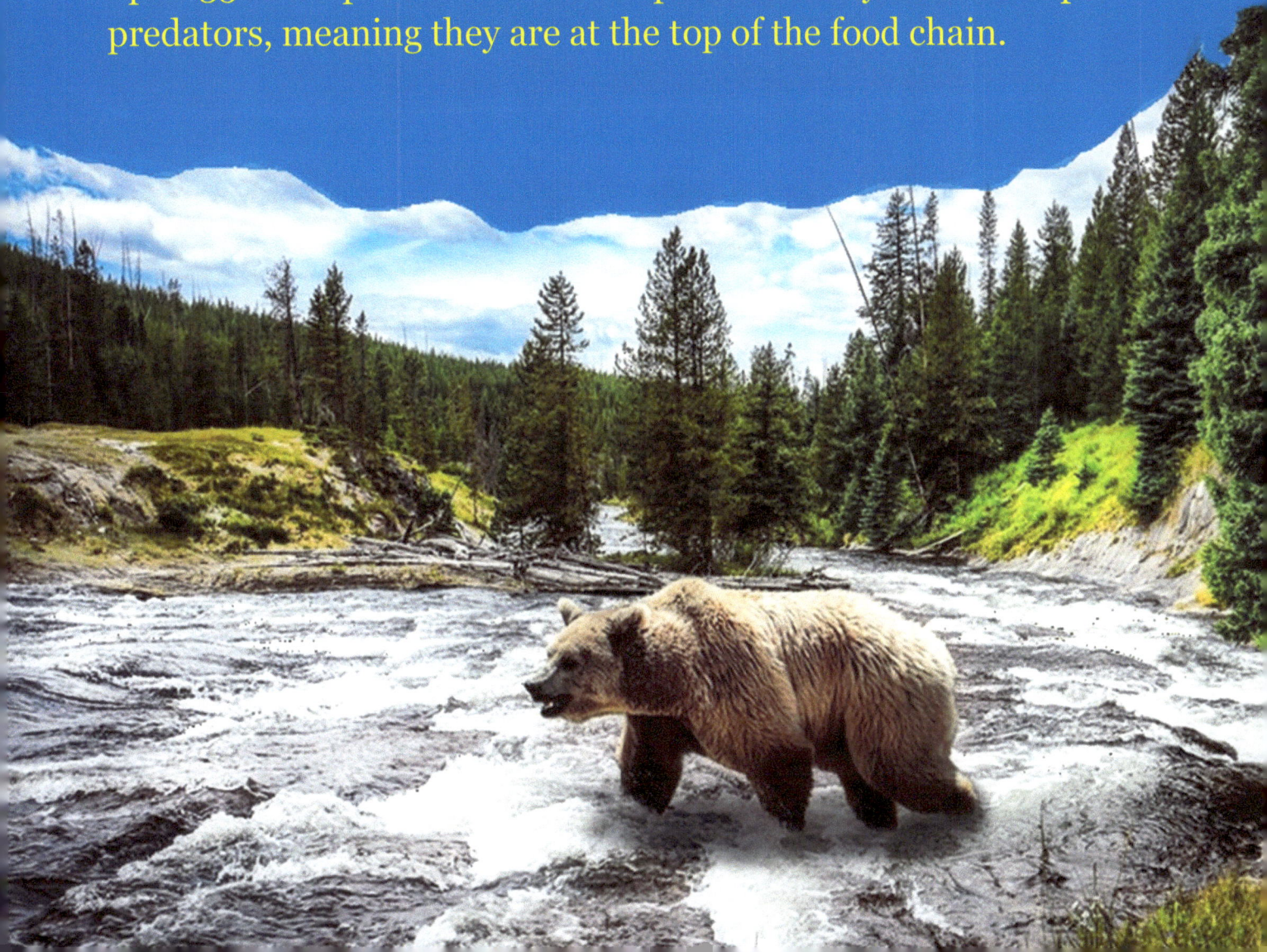

The Polar Bear is one of the biggest bears on earth. Male polar bears can weigh up to 1500 lbs. Female polar bears weigh about half as much as males. They like swimming and can swim constantly for days at a time. Polar bears keep warm thanks to the blubber under their skin. They can smell up to a mile away. Polar bears spend most of their time at sea. They can run 25 mph, and they can swim up to 10 mph. There's still a debate of whether the Kodiak bear or the polar bear is the biggest bear in the world. Polar bears are found in Alaska and arctic areas.

The North American Bison and Buffalo are sometimes confused as the same animal, but they are not. Bison have long hair on their backs, front, and a long beard. Bison are bigger than buffalo. They are the largest mammal in North America and weigh up to 2,000 pounds. Bison can run up to 35 miles per hour. They can jump 6 feet vertically and more than 7 feet horizontally. Bison calves are nicknamed red dogs, because of their orange-red color at birth.

Bald Eagles are very adaptive and live in just about every part of the world including the arctic regions. The largest bald eagles live in Alaska. They build the largest nest of any North American bird. The bald eagle is America's national bird.

The bald eagle gets their name due to their white hair on their head. They can fly up to 30 mph, and dive at speeds up to 100 mph. Male bald eagles are smaller than females. Eagles return to same nesting territory year after year.

Author Page

Billy Grinslott & Kinsey Marie Books

ISBN – 9781965098615

Thanks

www.ingramcontent.com/pod-product-compliance
Lightning Source LLC
Chambersburg PA
CBHW060853270326
41934CB00002B/118

9 781965 098615